Socks

Story by Janie Spaht Gill, Ph.D.
Illustrations by Elizabeth Lambson

Dominie Press, Inc.

Should I wear my
patchy socks,
my itchy and
my scratchy socks?

4

Should I wear
my messy socks?

Should I wear
my dressy socks?

Should I wear
my daisy socks?

Should I wear
my crazy socks?

Should I wear
my red and green socks?

Should I wear
my Halloween socks?

Should I wear
my tall socks?

18

Should I wear
my small socks?

20

Or should I wear
no socks at all?

Curriculum Extension Activities

Socks

- Have a "Crazy Sock" day, a day when the children wear unique socks to school. Also, they could decorate white socks at school using glitter, bows, ribbons, and beads.

- Have the children bring one of their socks to school and classify them according to color and the material they're made of. Make a bar graph depicting the results.

- Use this opportunity to discuss what a "pair of socks" means. Have ten children bring a pair of socks to school and place them before the class. Have the class count by two's to twenty. Discuss other things that come in pairs.

- Brainstorm a list of nouns beginning with the letter *s*. Have each child pick an *s* word to draw. Then have them write the word under the picture and put the *s* words in order, from heaviest to lightest.

About the Author

Dr. Janie Spaht Gill brings twenty-five years of teaching experience to her books for young children. During her career thus far, she has taught at every grade level, from kindergarten through college. Gill has a Ph.D. in reading education, with a minor in creative writing. She is currently residing in Lafayette, Louisiana with her husband, Richard. Her fresh, humorous topics are inspired by the things her students say in the classroom. Gill was voted the 1999-2000 Louisiana Elementary Teacher of the Year for her outstanding work in primary education.

Publisher: Raymond Yuen
Editorial Consultant: Adria F. Klein
Editor: Bob Rowland
Designer: Natalie Chupil
Illustrator: Elizabeth Lambson

Published by:

ᵱ Dominie Press, Inc.

1949 Kellogg Avenue
Carlsbad, California 92008 USA

www.dominie.com
(800) 232-4570

Softcover Edition ISBN 0-7685-2132-7
Library Bound Edition ISBN 0-7685-2440-7

Printed in Singapore by PH Productions Pte Ltd
1 2 3 4 5 6 PH 05 04 03

Dominie Level	Guided Reading	DeFord Assessment
6	D	3B